"What y~ ~ve crea~ ~es
here m~ ~ss ~ ~erence."

"Robert Glazer is paying it forward
one week at a time. With how
insightful these messages are, it's
easy to see why the Friday Forward
has such a massive following. You just
need to read them for yourself to believe
the hype. Each post oozes with passion, and
you gain a sense that he has a genuine passion
for helping those who read his words."

—US METRO

~ push~
front of my ~ ~
been stagnant for t~ ~
I hope you realize the great
impact some of these have
on your followers! I look
forward to your insights
each week, so thank
you for your continued
consistency and
inspiration. Cheers."
—ABBY O.

~R PODCAST

~m greetings from
~th Africa! Through
~y Forward message,
~e indeed become the
~ of our organizational
~nge for almost the last
~ started forwarding the
~o our staff every Friday."
—YESHITILA A. A.

~gs happening in my
~oices I am making.
~nk you, Bob."

"THANK YOU for the message this morning.
We're dealing with a problem with a great
customer right now that has sapped the
energy of our team this week, and your
note couldn't have been more timely.
I was happy to share it!"
—JOHN D.

~y Forward. I just sent it
~ here at [our fund] and
~ortfolio companies."
~GRANT G.

"Short, but packed with
great insights."
—JENNIFER M.

"Bob Glazer has become one of the finest business columnists writing today, and he's done it while building a truly great company, Acceleration Partners. You can get a taste of both from this wonderful book."

—Bo Burlingham, author of *Small Giants* and *Finish Big*

"Leaders who elevate both themselves and their people will see the greatest success in these turbulent times. In *Elevate*, Glazer demonstrates how the four elements of capacity, explored both separately and as part of an integrated whole, offer a blueprint for personal and professional achievement. On every page, Glazer's advice is both encouraging and realistic, and he masterfully combines real-world examples and clear framework for anyone to reach a higher level of achievement."

—Stew Friedman, Wharton School professor and author of *Total Leadership*

"This book is simply a masterpiece. It's an easy-to-read yet profoundly valuable guidebook to living a successful (as YOU define success), happy, and joy-filled life. Each and every page contains golden nuggets of wisdom within a system you can follow to blow past perceived self limits and accomplish more than you might presently think possible. Best of all, Glazer equips you to improve the lives of others as you help lead them to do the same. And—by all means—buy a copy of this book for your children, grandchildren, your business team, and everyone else who you want to help be nine steps ahead of the game...in a ten-step game."

—Bob Burg, coauthor of the Go-Giver Series and author of *Adversaries into Allies*

ELEVATE

Push Beyond Your

Limits and Unlock Success

in Yourself and Others

ROBERT GLAZER

IGNITE READS
spark impact in just one hour

simple truths
Small books. BIG IMPACT.

Photo Credits
Internal images © page xvi, Thomas Barwick/Getty Images; page xxii, Azri Suratmin/Getty Images; page 26, Xsandra/Getty Images; page 28, RichVintage/Getty Images; page 38, Westend61/Getty Images; page 64, Mint Images/Tim Pannell/Getty Images; page 70, Noelia Ramon - TellingLife/Getty Images; page 86, contrastaddict/Getty Images; page 92, svetikd/Getty Images;
Internal images on the end sheets and pages xii, xx, 6, 12, 18, 32, 44, 50, 58, 76, 78, 82, 94, 101, 102, 114, 118, and 122 have been provided by Pexels, Pixabay, or Unsplash; these images are licensed under CC0 Creative Commons and have been released by the author for public use.

Published by Simple Truths, an imprint of Sourcebooks
P.O. Box 4410, Naperville, Illinois 60567-4410
(630) 961-3900
sourcebooks.com

Printed and bound in China.
OGP 10 9 8 7 6 5 4 3 2 1

For everyone who knows deep down
they can be more.

For Chloe, Max, and Zach. You each
inspire me to be better every day.

Table of

Contents

ELEVATE

verb

to raise or lift (something)
up to a higher position or
raise to a more important or
impressive level.

CAPACITY

noun

the ability or power to do,
experience, or understand
something.

Foreword

BY STEWART D. FRIEDMAN

Professor of Management Practice, Emeritus, the Wharton School, University of Pennsylvania, author of *Total Leadership: Be a Better Leader, Have a Richer Life*

Since the 1980s, I've been in the business of discovering and sharing practical, evidence-based knowledge about how to build leadership capacity in all parts of life. In the early days of this work, the concept of leaders pursuing integration among the different parts of their lives was far out of the mainstream. It's inspiring to see that the zeitgeist has changed, and that the legitimate demand for useful knowledge about creating harmony in our lives has exploded. A generation of thought leaders are emerging to fill the need in this era; they are thought leaders who bring great talent and rich experience to bear on articulating wisdom that rests on the understanding that leadership in business is no longer just about business, it's about life.

Bob Glazer is one such thinker. In *Elevate*, he shares readily applicable ideas for how to understand and cultivate the interconnected elements that make us who we are as distinct individuals, what I refer to as the domain of the private self—our spiritual, intellectual, physical, and emotional lives. He shows how these four pieces, explored both separately and as part of an integrated whole, offer a blueprint for personal and professional achievement. On the foundation of a philosophy rooted in a commitment to continually learning, Glazer boosts our understanding of the importance of knowing what we want. This knowledge is always hard won; it takes courage, because to identify your core values requires choice, which is often accompanied by anxiety. On every page, Glazer's advice is both encouraging and realistic, just as his particular emphasis on raising expectations is both smart and optimistic. His hopeful view, which I share, is that we all have more capacity than we believe. We just have to pursue this idea and enlist the support of those around us who want to see us succeed in producing value for our world.

The good news is that this can be done, and this book helps point the way. Leaders who elevate both themselves and their people will see the greatest success in these turbulent times. So hold on for the great ride that Bob Glazer is going to take you on in this zestful read of a book. He's curated a terrific bunch of resources and examples you can use to get yourself to the next level of leadership capacity. It may not be comfortable or easy, but it will surely be worth your time and attention to obtain this wisdom and try it out for yourself. You are bound to see returns not just for you, but, more importantly, for the people who matter to you in your work, in your family, and in your community as you seek to make your contribution as a leader striving for harmony in our fractious world.

Introduction

"If you have the courage to begin,
you have the courage to succeed."

—DAVID VISCOTT

Have you ever wondered why some individuals are consistently able to achieve at such a high level? They are always pushing forward and hitting their goals. They seem to be doing more with less, while the rest of us spin our wheels and don't make as much progress. The same is true with organizations. It might be comforting to believe they have some advantage, when the truth is they have found a way to become an elevated version of themselves.

In 2015, I started sending an inspirational email every Friday to the people at my company, Acceleration Partners, which I later named "Friday Forward." Rather than focus the content on business-related topics, I hoped to provide inspiration around the concept of personal improvement and growth. My goal was to encourage our employees to want to achieve more in all areas of their lives. I wanted to help them challenge their self-limiting beliefs and realize their true potential, something that very much aligned to my core values.

I thought my Friday emails would be skimmed, at best, and maybe even ignored. To my surprise, employees told me they looked forward to the messages each week and shared them with friends and family. The weekly emails also had a noticeable impact within our company, as people started taking action and applying the different concepts in their work and lives. In just a few short years, these weekly messages had spread to over one hundred thousand people across fifty countries and were shared regularly across and within organizations of all kinds.

In creating and sharing the Friday Forward emails, my initial goal was to inspire and motivate others. However, I soon came to realize a deeper truth.

By tackling these concepts and having the discipline to write about them each week, I was pushing myself to perform better and grow my *own* capacity, including my ability to achieve and perform consistently at a higher level. Inspiration of others was the catalyst, and my journey of personal growth and achievement was the effect.

I could see my Friday Forward messages were helping others in life and at work. Our team members began reaching new personal and professional heights simultaneously. They were running races, getting healthier, committing to more quality time with family,

traveling abroad as well as outside their comfort zones, and creating positive examples for one another. By taking a holistic approach to inspiring our team, we saw a higher return on investment than we did by just helping them get better at their current jobs.

The same was true of people who would write back to me each week from across the world and share their stories and experiences of growth and achievement.

I could tell I was making a difference, but I wasn't as clear about how. So I dug into the themes of my writing and quickly realized the patterns that illuminated the four elements of capacity building. Soon, I had a simple framework for changing my life, growing my business, and improving both the lives of employees and strangers.

Be forewarned, this isn't a scientific book with academic studies and theories. It's a book full of real-world results, time-tested principles, and actionable advice designed in a format that you can keep on your desk or bedside table and dive into at different points based on where you are on your capacity-building journey at any point in time.

I am excited to share this framework, which has served as a personal road map to higher achievement. I believe it is the key to elevating and achieving things both in life and business that you never thought possible.

1.

What Is Capacity Building?

"The difference between what we do and what we are capable of doing would suffice to solve most of the world's problems."

—MAHATMA GANDHI

In its purest definition, capacity building is the method by which individuals seek, acquire, and develop the skills and abilities to consistently perform at a higher level in pursuit of their innate potential.

High achievers across all spectrums of life and business have found continuous ways to build their capacity at faster rates than their peers and use that extra capacity to stay ahead of the pack and achieve at the highest level; it's how they elevate. People who consistently elevate, or "elevaters," have a competitive advantage, but it's one that you can replicate.

To illustrate what capacity building looks like in real life, I'll share the story of an inquisitive high school student who became enamored with travel—with Asia in particular—after spending a year abroad. He set his sights on getting into Princeton, which is known for its strong East Asian studies program.

When a misguided guidance counselor told him he had no hope of getting accepted, he rightfully got riled, took the counselor's lack of faith in him as a direct challenge, and did the hard work to get himself accepted.[1]

Years later, after starting his own business, he decided to take a trip abroad to get centered. To enjoy the trip and live in the moment, he was forced to set up processes for virtual work and delegation, because he had no employees.

At age twenty-nine, he turned the experiences from that trip and his outsourcing exploits into a book and pitched it to publishers. The first twenty-five publishers rejected it. The twenty-sixth surprised him by offering a contract.

When he asked them why, the publisher told him,

"We can understand why publishers have rejected this work, but we aren't betting on the book, we are betting on *you*. We believe you will do anything and everything you can to make the book successful."[2]

That book was *The 4-Hour Workweek*, which went on to sell over 1.3 million copies in thirty-five languages and launched the career of Tim Ferriss.

Dismissed by many as a get-rich-quick book on marketing and outsourcing, for many in the Gen X/Y demographic cohort, *The 4-Hour Workweek* was really a new manifesto on capacity building and human potential—a new philosophy for how to live a more intentional and fulfilling life.

Tim lives and breathes capacity building and is fascinated by others who do the same; he systematically breaks down and analyzes how top performers achieve success. He's experimented frequently on his own body. He's learned to speak five languages. He's the first American to hold a Guinness record in tango spins. He learned angel investing and backed a few small companies such as Uber, Facebook, Twitter, Alibaba, and Shopify. His podcast has had more than three hundred million downloads, and he's now written five number one *New York Times* and *Wall Street Journal* bestsellers.

Tim's commitment to personal development is insatiable, and it has led him not only to achieve incredible things in life but also to inspire countless others to do the same.

Not bad for a guy whose guidance counselor thought he wasn't Ivy League material.

To be clear, capacity building is not about doing more. It's about doing more of the right things. In fact, the art of the capacity-building process is knowing where you need to invest your energy and where you need to pull away.

As the legendary management guru Peter Drucker once wrote, "There is surely nothing quite so useless as doing with great efficiency what should not be done at all."

Capacity building is similar to a developing a muscle. It doesn't happen overnight. I may be inspired to lift a heavy weight, but only after weeks of consistent commitment, work, and incremental improvement will I have built up the strength and physical capacity to do so. Suddenly, I have the capacity to do what I could not do before. Inspiration is valuable, but it's not enough to affect real change. That requires follow-though and commitment.

In my own journey and in speaking with hundreds of others who have made meaningful and sustained changes to their lives, I have identified four essential elements of capacity building: spiritual, intellectual, physical, and emotional. These four elements are fundamental and are present in nearly every aspect of self-improvement.

I will go into each of these elements in much greater detail in the next few chapters, but here is a brief overview of each:

1. Spiritual capacity is about understanding who you are, what you want most, and the standards you want to live by each day.

2. Intellectual capacity is about how you improve your ability to think, learn, plan, and execute with discipline.

3. Physical capacity is your health, well-being, and physical performance.

4. Emotional capacity is how you react to challenging situations, your emotional mindset, and the quality of your relationships.

Capacity building starts with understanding these four interconnected elements and then developing them individually and simultaneously.

Think of each element as a chamber of an inflatable ball separated into four sections, and each section

CAPACITY DEVELOPMENT

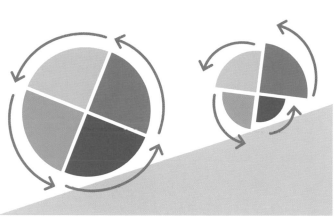

can be filled individually with a dense gas. The bigger the ball becomes, the more energy and mass it will have, resulting in optimal momentum as it rolls. It will perform best when all the chambers grow in tandem rather than one section getting too big at the expense of the others. If one chamber is bigger or another is underinflated, the ball will not roll evenly. Instead of gaining speed and building momentum, it's going to wobble awkwardly and get off track.

These chambers are also leaky and constantly

need filling. Similar to tires on your car, they need continuous maintenance to ensure they have the right pressure and are in balance. Balance is often hard to identify, but being aware of imbalance—and identifying exactly which chamber is slowing you down—is often the key to keeping you on course.

Building physical capacity offers the most concrete example between *increased effort* and *improved outcomes*. You see that if you run a little bit more each day, it becomes easier as your conditioning improves. Likewise, if you lift a little more weight each day, you can soon lift what you could not just a few months or weeks before. The process is the same for things that are not physical.

Focusing on building capacity within ourselves and our teams is one of the core principles that we have used at Acceleration Partners to build an award-winning culture.

A leader's goal should be to inspire and elevate expectations so that team members can simultaneously improve in all areas of their lives, including leadership, time management, prioritization, decision-making, self-awareness, and self-confidence. These abilities have a domino effect. When you improve in one area, you begin to improve in all, and one of the most important outcomes in capacity building is the exponential effect it has on others, including friends, family, and those whom you lead. It has the effect of lifting while you climb—as you build your own capacity and achieve more, you develop the ability to help others do the same.

It's a virtuous cycle and benefits everyone involved.

By focusing on these elements, you'll be on a path to build your own capacity to elevate and support others in their journeys as well.

2.

Build Your Spiritual Capacity

"Becoming a leader is synonymous with becoming yourself. It's precisely that simple, and it's also that difficult."

—WARREN BENNIS

The term *spiritual* is often used in the context of religion or things that are intangible, but in the context of capacity building, it means something different.

At its core, spiritual capacity is about understanding who you are and what you want most for your life. It's the process of developing your North Star and the principles that guide your actions and shape your major decisions. Building your spiritual capacity is really a journey of self-actualization, a path of discovery about the unique motivations that you have within you. It's the motor that is driving you, either unconsciously or consciously.

Great companies have clear visions of where they want to go, an enduring purpose, as well as clearly established core values. These same principles apply to living a great life.

With a company, the vision is usually easier to decipher. It's often the reason that the company was started in the first place (e.g., the founder wanted to disrupt transportation or eradicate cancer). The core values are often developed over time, as they represent the collective values of team members.

With individuals, the inverse is true; it's easier for us to first identify our core values. It's very unlikely you entered this world as a baby understanding and able to clearly articulate the purpose or vision for your life. This is a concept many of us don't begin to contemplate until our thirties or forties, but the sooner you start, the better.

CORE VALUES

Your core values are the principles that are most important to you. They serve as your guideposts or "swim lanes." Consciously or subconsciously, they drive many of your most important decisions, such as your chosen vocation, whom you marry, and where you choose to live. When you are doing things aligned with your values, you feel energized. When you aren't, it drains your energy, and you feel out of place. When you are clear on your values, you know how to make faster and better decisions.

If you can't clearly articulate your own personal

core values, you are navigating life without a GPS. Sure, you might get to the right place(s) eventually though trial and error, but you are going to take a lot of unnecessary and avoidable wrong turns along the way, wasting valuable time and resources.

Getting to your core values requires working on yourself and taking some quiet time to reflect on what is most important to you. When are you happy? When are you drained? In what situations do you do well? In what situations do you struggle?

Ask the same questions of your partner, friends, and family. You might even read your old report cards or your performance evaluations to search for clues.

Soon, you will begin to see similar themes, and consistent concepts or words will reveal themselves, such as *independent*, *fair*, *compassionate*, *self-reliant*, *dependable*, *passionate*, *consistent*.

Begin to create a list, and then start to "kill and combine" until you have narrowed down the list to four or five principles you feel represent you best or are nonnegotiable principles in your life. As you get closer to the truth, you might see a difference between how you felt or performed during times when you were able to live your values and times when you were forced to go against or suppress them.

Take your final list, and put it on your desk as a starting point. You can always continue to tweak it over time.

CORE PURPOSE AND WHY

If core values help you navigate your daily journey, your core purpose helps you understand your ultimate destination. Think of it as the topic sentence for your life, a clear direction supported by your values as pillars.

Ask one hundred people if they can articulate their core purpose, and ninety-eight will have not really thought about it or have clarity. The other two will

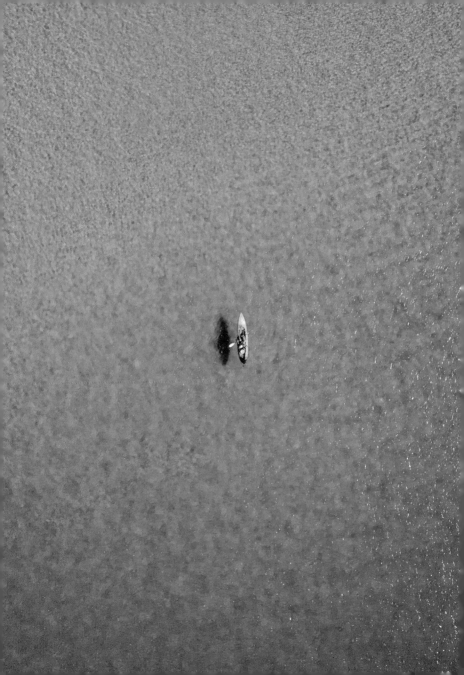

tell you clearly, and I can almost guarantee that they have an elevated focus. Most importantly, it is in the service of that purpose that they spend the majority of their time and energy.

For some, there is a clear formative event in their life that drives their purpose, and it often originates from a place of pain. For example, if you had a hard time reading as a child, you may become a champion of literacy. If your family suffered an injustice, you may have dedicated your life to being a champion of the law or human rights. The connection is clear.

For the rest of us, it's not as obvious. However, the emerging concept of discovering your why, made popular by author and motivational speaker Simon Sinek, has helped many to discover their purpose under a different name. The theory is you are driven by your why, whether you know it or not. I see core purpose and why as one and the same.

In fall 2013, I attended an Entrepreneurs' Organization (EO) event and joined a session by author and serial entrepreneur Ridgely Goldsborough on discovering your why.

In his presentation, Ridgely explained that we each have a why—a core purpose that underpins everything we do across our business and personal lives—and he shared the archetypes of nine different whys.

Ridgely asked for volunteers, and within minutes of talking with them and asking questions, he had identified their why. I vividly recall the shocked, vulnerable, and even relieved look in people's eyes as their purpose became clear. It was incredibly powerful.

Then and there, I realized that I, too, needed to know my why.

Later that day, I chased down Ridgely and asked him to help me discover my why, which turned out to be "Find a better way and share it." (Some of the tools we used are available to you at the end of the chapter.)

It's hard to explain what it feels like when you have both clarity and permission to be who you are and who you have likely always been. It's as if someone just gave you the instructional manual for your own life, which was left out of the box at the factory.

Suddenly, the repeated patterns of my life were illuminated clearly. It explained my behavior as far back as the age of six, when my mom would ask me to clean my room and I'd rearrange it instead. It also explains my leadership style, my creation of Friday Forward, and even my desire to write this book. It became obvious to me that I did well in situations where I had the opportunity to improve or grow something or to impact change. Finding a way to drive positive change fuels my energy. Conversely, if I can't make things better and am forced to simply follow established rules or processes, I become frustrated, disengaged, and drained of energy.

Armed with this knowledge, I began to align my long term goals and actions with these newly discovered principles. I set a goal to spend eighty percent (or more) of my time and effort on things that aligned with my core purpose or values. I began to rid my plate of everything that didn't align with my purpose and to double down on everything that did, such as Friday Forward. I started saying no to existing relationships and commitments that no longer made sense.

This process elevated my life to an entirely new level.

Developing your spiritual capacity is essential to creating alignment between what you want most and your daily actions, something most of us struggle with repeatedly (a challenge that will be addressed in the next chapter). Without that alignment, you may be running really hard in the wrong direction or obtain the appearance of success that feels inauthentic or unfulfilling. Even though you can build capacity in each of the elements, that energy and effort may be misplaced. You might set the wrong goals (intellectual capacity), continue toxic relationships (emotional capacity), or demonstrate reliance (physical capacity) in something you should have never started. An example of someone who has created this alignment brilliantly is Ray Dalio, the founder and CEO of Bridgewater. He published an incredible book, *Principles: Life and Work*, which defines the core principles and values by which he runs both his life and his business, and they are fundamentally the same.

Developing your spiritual capacity is an ongoing process. The elements of who you are and what you want most will inevitably change throughout your life as your experiences and learnings impact your chosen direction. If you haven't started this process or it is one you are still working on, I have included some helpful resources that I have taken advantage of on my own journey.

ACTION STEPS

Getting Started

▶ Think about times in your life when you have done well and times when you've struggled. What did those situations have in common? Write a few down, and circle the words/concepts that overlapped.

▶ Order a copy of *True North: Discover Your Authentic Leadership* by Bill George and/or *Man's Search for Meaning* by Viktor Frankl.

▶ Take one or more of the tests below that will help you asses your personality, strengths, and natural tendencies:

- Strengths Finder: https://www.gallupstrengthscenter.com/

- DISC Behavior Assessment: https://www.discprofile.com /what-is-disc/overview/

- Total Leadership Assessment: http://www.totalleadership .org/resources/assessments/ (Assess Your Skills)

Advanced

▶ Visit one of these resources to get started on discovering your why.

- The Why Stack: https://www.thewhystack.com/

- Start with Why: https://startwithwhy.com/

- WHY Institute, where you can find the nine archetypes: http://whyinstitute.com/

▶ Download the Whole Life Dashboard (https://www.fridayfwd.com/wld) for a detailed exercise on discovering your core values.

▶ Write down a few paragraphs of your own obituary. How do you want to be remembered? Your answer will likely contain several words that are part of your core purpose or core values.

To read more inspirational stories about building your spiritual capacity, visit www.fridayfwd.com /spiritual

Scan me with your camera phone for more resources!

SPIRITUAL

3.

Build Your Intellectual Capacity

Intellectual capacity is about how you improve your ability to think, learn, plan, and execute with discipline. It is closely correlated with the area of your brain called the *frontal lobe*, which acts as the control panel for many of your executive functions.

Think of intellectual capacity as your personal processor/operating system that can be continuously upgraded to perform the same tasks smarter, faster, or more efficiently than before. The greater your intellectual capacity, the greater your level of achievement with the same or less expenditure of energy.

This element of capacity building can offer the greatest opportunity for immediate gains, but it also requires the most discipline.

COMMITMENT TO IMPROVEMENT

"The measure of success is not whether you have a tough problem to deal with, but whether it's the same problem you had last year."

—JOHN FOSTER DULLES

Your intelligence is not fixed and can always improve, but sadly, many people believe that they were born with a predetermined level. Even worse, this belief may have come from being told this by a parent, teacher, or authority figure when they were younger.

High achievers know that this is a falsehood. They see the tangible and dramatic improvement that comes with increased intellectual capacity.

It may sound obvious, but the first step to increasing your intellectual capacity is believing that you can.

Stanford psychologist Carol Dweck coined the

term *growth mindset*. She became interested in students' attitudes about failure, and it led to a twenty-year discovery project. She found a profound difference between two types of mindsets, and she defined those as a *growth mindset* and a *fixed mindset*.

A fixed mindset is one where you assume your character, intelligence, and creative ability are static things that you come prepackaged with and can't change in any meaningful way. The danger of this mindset is that if you believe that something is fixed—your level of intelligence, for instance—it has negative consequences for how you learn.

Conversely, a growth mindset implies you always have the ability to learn and increase your capacity. A person with a growth mindset believes that hard work, challenges, and failures help you to grow and stretch your potential.

Here are some characteristics of the two mindsets, courtesy of my son's class. I found these mindset-shifting affirmations on five posters within his classroom.

FIXED MINDSET   GROWTH MINDSET

FIXED MINDSET	GROWTH MINDSET
"I can't do this."	"I'm going to train my brain in how to do this."
"I'll never get this."	"I will find resources to help me."
"I hate when I mess up."	"I am resilient and learn from my mistakes."
"I hate when I'm corrected."	"Feedback helps me improve."
"I'm so dumb."	"I'm learning! I just need more practice."

Intellectual capacity is highly correlated with a commitment to lifelong learning. It's the product of an open mind that can see multiple points of view, voracious reading, intellectual curiosity, and a desire to problem solve and acquire new knowledge.

In 2005, I met an energetic and entrepreneurial MIT student named Drew who was working on an online test prep business and was thinking about how to leverage affiliate marketing. He had an obvious love for learning and always asked great questions; he really wanted to understand everything he didn't know. I later learned that when he realized how much he needed to learn about business as an undergrad engineer, he would buy the top three or four books on Amazon for that subject (i.e., marketing), take a folding chair to the roof, and spend most of the weekend reading. This allowed him to upgrade his knowledge base and "processor" simultaneously; he could make decisions faster and understand a topic better than just a week before.

A year or two after we first met, Drew sent me a

demo CD for a new business, which initially seemed to me to be just another online backup service in an already a crowded market. That product was called Dropbox, and I used it while writing this book. The founder, Drew Houston, is worth over $2 billion and is still a voracious learner to this day. Drew is driven to elevate.

One of the best ways to grow your intellectual and emotional capacity at the same time is to form or join a mastermind group. A mastermind group is very different from a traditional networking group where people are there foremost to get introductions or leads for their benefit. The mastermind concept was originally presented by Napoleon Hill, who defined it as "the coordination of knowledge and effort of two or more people, who work toward a definite purpose, in the spirit of harmony." Said more simply, it's a group whose purpose is to help one another learn and grow, both individually and collectively.

The concept of a mastermind group is the same

framework as many self-help organizations, such as Alcoholics Anonymous. It's also the basis for the forum concept that is the cornerstone of several business peer advisory organizations such as Young Presidents' Organization (YPO), Entrepreneurs' Organization (EO), Vistage, and Mastermind Talks. Mastermind Talks has seen more than seventeen thousand people apply to the annual event since Jayson Gaignard started it in 2013, but the acceptance rate is just 0.4 percent—lower than Harvard's.

Mastermind groups or forums foster many of the principles within multiple elements of capacity building. They also operate under strict confidentiality so that people feel comfortable being vulnerable and sharing their experiences to best learn from one another.

If a mastermind group seems like too big of a commitment, invest time in building your network on a one-to-one basis, with a focus on creating value with like-minded individuals (*not* just collecting business cards or asking for favors or leads).

You might also seek out a mentor who can act as your personal coach, business coach, or both. Many elevaters also create a de facto personal board of advisors who they reach out to for key decisions and feedback.

We all have blind spots. Some people are just more open than others to having them pointed out. Think about Olympic athletes. They are already the best in the world, yet they retain multiple coaches to push them to continually improve and remain elite. However, I have met many mediocre athletes and business leaders who think they know everything and feel they don't need any coaching or feedback. They will continue to be mediocre until they change their approach.

Keep in mind the best feedback is often uncomfortable. An amazing example of this can be gleaned from a story about how Sheryl Sandberg gave feedback to fellow employee Kim Scott early in her career at Google.

Sandberg mentioned to Scott that she used the word *um* too much in a presentation she had just given and suggested she hire a speaking coach to help her improve. When Scott brushed off the feedback, Sandberg told her, in a caring but honest way, "You know, Kim, I can tell I'm not really getting through to you. I'm going to have to be clearer here. When you say 'um' every third word, it makes you sound stupid."[3] Sandberg then went on to offer Kim both support and coaching to correct the behavior.

Sandberg's feedback not only got Scott's attention, but in the years since, Scott established a firm called Candor, Inc. and is a now a sought-after keynote speaker and bestselling author of *Radical Candor*.

Most of us give the impression that we don't want feedback that makes us uncomfortable, so people don't give it to us. Then we just repeat the same mistakes rather than learn from them.

To grow, you need to learn. To learn, you need to know where you can improve. To improve, you need to

be self-aware. It's all a virtuous cycle that begins with believing that you can always get better and being open to being shown where and how.

BEING PROACTIVE

"It has long since come to my attention that people of accomplishment rarely sat back and let things happen to them. They went out and happened to things."

—ELINOR SMITH

Many of our choices in life revolve around the core decision to be reactive or proactive in any given situation. I can't stress enough that being reactive is rarely a recipe for success.

In 2005, I was working at a start-up and was completely miserable. With a two-year-old child to provide for and another on the way, I was determined to have two to three years of continuous professional employment on my resume. Yet the company's leadership was the opposite of inspirational; it was discouraging and demotivational.

Later that year, I went to lunch with my friend, Al Chase. During lunch, I shared with him my situation and why I felt that the responsible choice was to stay for a few years to gain operating experience and prove I was not a job hopper.

Al listened and then looked me square in the eye and said, "My friend, I give you permission to leave." Seeing the confused look on my face, he explained his advice. "You have got to do what's right for you."

This was a pivotal moment for me and a great example of how to inspire someone by pushing them outside their comfort zone—a key principal to be discussed later. Al's advice turned a lightbulb on in my head: I had accepted the middle lane and put what I wanted most on hold. I wasn't learning, and I wasn't getting better. My capacity had plateaued.

Shortly after, I left and tapped into my entrepreneurial passion by starting two companies, one of which was Acceleration Partners. That was over eleven years ago.

A huge part of being proactive is looking forward, even if the horizon is not clear or you have sunk a lot into your current situation, making you double down on a bad decision. Moving forward requires not looking over your shoulder, other than to learn from mistakes. It also requires focusing energy on what you can control, not on macro trends and uncontrollable circumstances.

I can't control that it's raining today, but I can control if I am going to let the rain ruin my plans. Likewise, I can't control the stock market, but I can decide how I will act when different outcomes occur.

When given the choice, choose to take action and keep the capacity ball moving downhill—momentum usually builds upon itself. When in doubt, you can always fall back on one of the greatest marketing slogans of all time: "Just Do It."

In life, we regret the things we didn't do and the chances we didn't take far more than the ones we did.

SETTING SHORT-TERM AND LONG-TERM GOALS

"If you don't know where you're going, you might not get there."

—YOGI BERRA

Achievement is the high-level attainment of goals, a concept I prefer over the more common term *success*, which is far more subjective. For example, consider the "successful" business executive whose spouse is close to leaving him or whose kids don't talk to him. Most would not consider such a person successful. Achievement, on the other hand, relies on having clarity about what is most important and making decisions accordingly.

Goal setting is where spiritual and intellectual

capacity intersect; think of it as "what you want" meeting "how you get there." I once believed I was great at setting goals. I would set a bunch of one-year goals and hit them regularly. However, because I wasn't aligning these short-term goals with my long-term goals, I wasn't moving in a meaningful or specific direction.

Long-term goals should be derived from your core values and/or your core purpose, because they are what you want most. A way to audit goals is to make sure you really understand the *why* for each. Therefore, you don't need to derive purpose from your goals, because your goals help you serve your purpose and values. For example, do you want a beach home because it means that you have made it? Or do you want it because it's a place to spend quality time with your family? If it's about your family but none of them like the beach, reaching this goal likely won't make you happier or more fulfilled. Eventually, I came to understand my one-year goals needed to

align with and emanate from my five-year goals, my ten-year goals, and my lifetime goals. Quarterly and annual goals became small down payments on what I wanted most.

There is a great story about Warren Buffett that conveys the importance of focus in goal setting and in the realm of intellectual capacity. As the story goes, Buffett heard his personal airplane pilot, Mike Flint, talking about his long-term goals and priorities. After he was done, Buffett suggested to Flint that he conduct the following exercise:

▶ STEP 1: Write down your top twenty-five career goals on a single piece of paper.

▶ STEP 2: Circle only your top five options.

▶ STEP 3: Put the top five on one list and the remaining twenty on a second list.

When Flint commented that he would continue to work on the second list intermittently, Buffett interjected, saying, "No. You've got it wrong, Mike. Everything you didn't circle just became your avoid-at-all-cost list. No matter what, these things get no attention from you until you've succeeded with your top five."

The implication is that the other twenty goals would distract him from accomplishing his top five most important goals.

Taking Warren Buffett's approach to goal setting and focus a step further, I suggest making that twenty-five-to-five list across four dimensions of your life: personal, professional, family, and community.

A question I often hear asked is, "Should I be meeting one hundred percent of my goals?" Conventional wisdom says that if you are meeting all your goals, you probably aren't aiming high enough. That said, you also don't want to aim too high and feel as if you aren't accomplishing anything. It's a delicate balance.

There are several ways to find that balance. One is to define a minimum threshold (e.g., "I want to lose ten to twenty pounds" or "I want to save at least $1,000 a month"). This way, even if you come up short of the stretch goal, you still win.

Another strategy is to focus on repeatable daily or weekly inputs (habits) that will get you where you want to go. This gives you something to measure each week and helps you hold yourself accountable. Instead of an annual goal for health, you might instead commit to working out three mornings a week or taking a fifteen-minute break every day.

In this way, the input is the goal rather than an outcome that may seem initially out of reach. For example, while one person gets on Facebook for thirty minutes a day, another commits to invest that same time writing a book. At the end of three months, the first person is much wiser about their friends' vacations and the food they are eating but has nothing otherwise to show for that time. The other person has drafted the first thirty to forty pages of the book they always wanted to write.

Whatever goal-setting approach you take, what's most important is that you know when you have met your goals. This is where the SMART acronym comes into play. Your goals should be specific, measurable, attainable, realistic, and timely.

Don't give yourself wiggle room to believe you have accomplished something that you really didn't. After all, you're more likely to meet goals if you have a certain level of consistency and accountability.

ESTABLISHING ROUTINE, HABITS, AND ACCOUNTABILITY

*"Either you run the day, or
the day runs you."*

—JIM ROHN

Each day, the path to increasing your intellectual capacity will be tested. This is where discipline and planning are essential and the concepts of routine, habit, and accountability become increasingly important. *Remember, your schedule reflects your priorities.*

There are very few world-class performers who begin the day lounging around or leave the day to chance. They have a routine. Routines are powerful forces, and many great leaders know that beginning the morning well can set the tone for the whole day.

Unfortunately, many of us start our days reactively. By taking control of your mornings and beginning

your day on offense, you can ground yourself to your goals and align your actions to them.

I can tell you from experience that your entire day will change, and eventually, your entire life will change as well.

It wasn't easy for me to become a morning person and wake up at or before 6:00 a.m. each day. However, gradually I designed a routine that gave me more energy and intention without any distractions. I began to enjoy my mornings so much that I was psyched to get out of bed, waking up with the same energy and enthusiasm I have when heading to the airport for a vacation.

My morning routine is structured heavily on the format outlined by Hal Elrod in his book *The Miracle Morning*, which has developed a cult following. Hal suggests devoting a minimum of thirty to sixty minutes to the six SAVERS activities:

- **S**ilence (meditation)
- **A**ffirmations
- **V**isualization
- **E**xercising
- **R**eading
- **S**cribing (journaling)

Instead of beginning your day worried about your forty-two new emails, you begin with gratitude and powerful affirmations. In the process, you'll recommit to what you want most at the start of each day.

Eventually, your psyche will change.

One of the biggest objections to an early morning routine comes from parents of young kids who are already short on sleep. We heard this from many of my employees at Acceleration Partners.

For them, I offered a simple challenge. Start with getting up just fifteen minutes earlier, so you'll have fifteen minutes of quiet. Waking up with screaming kids as your alarm clock or to some situation that requires your parenting attention does not help you start your day with a positive, productive mindset.

If you're able to wake up just fifteen minutes earlier than your household, it will make a big difference.

Putting yourself first is something most of us don't do well. But you need to in order to be your best self for those around you. If you wake up cranky, reactively pandering to everyone else's needs, you're simply not going to perform at a high level.

Having a routine can also improve your discipline and directional habits overall. For example, on Tuesday, I draft the Friday Forward message for the week. On Wednesday, I edit the changes and pick an image to use. Thursday, I set it up to send. This process has become automatic; I don't need reminders.

Creating Friday Forward became a *keystone habit*—a habit that improved and reinforced other habits in my life.[4] These changes enabled me to hit new benchmarks of achievement, including running an Olympic triathlon, writing three books, biking from London to Paris in twenty-four hours, expanding my business globally, and accomplishing other goals that previously seemed entirely unobtainable.

Change didn't happen overnight; it was the compounding effect of many smaller changes in my life. Habit guru James Clear calls this "the 1 percent rule," illuminating how 1 percent improvements compound and accumulate into significant advantages over time as the aggregation of marginal gains. In

Atomic Habits, he even did the math to show that if you can get 1 percent better each day for one year, you'll end up thirty-seven times better by the time you're done.

Last but not least, you need accountability. Even if you know what you want and you are proactive, determined, and focused, you are going to slip. You are going to lose motivation or get off track.

True leaders hold others accountable and want to be held accountable themselves.

There are a variety of different ways to ensure accountability. The first is to team up with an accountability partner, group, or coach. Many people who elevate even get calls from a coach in the morning to check up on their progress and have predetermined consequences if goals are not met.

The second way is self-accountability, which is best accomplished through daily journaling. Journaling is reflective and will make you very aware of what you have and have not done. It's self-motivation and regulation—no one likes to write down the same thing day after day and see that he can't follow though.

Some people even hold themselves accountable by making their goals public. Jack Daly, a professional sales coach and speaker, puts all his goals on his business website. Doing this establishes a very high degree of accountability—and he almost always hits his targets.

If you follow the steps above, you will begin to elevate while feeling less overwhelmed and more energized. Your increased intellectual capacity will allow you to accomplish much more than you ever thought possible.

ACTION STEPS

Getting Started

▶ Get up fifteen minutes earlier. Do not look at email, news, or television for the first thirty minutes of your day. Read, write, think, or exercise during that time instead.

▶ Put down a deposit for something you have been wanting to do. This could be a payment for an event, an airline ticket, or an educational course. What's most important is that it puts a stake in the ground.

▶ Pick the three most important things to accomplish today and do them before noon.

Advanced

▶ Start keeping a journal. If you have never kept a journal before and want structure, check out the Five Minute Journal (https://www.intelligentchange.com), the best starter journal I have found.

▶ Set ten-, five-, three-, and one-year goals across the following dimensions: personal, professional, community, and family. Remember to make all your goals SMART: specific, measurable, attainable, realistic, and timely. (Note: Be very clear about whether you've reached your goal. For example, "running long distance" is not a SMART goal; "completing a half-marathon by January 2020" is.)

▶ If you have children, set annual family goals together so they learn how to set goals and hold themselves accountable. My children's goals have ranged from "Complete the high ropes course at camp" to "Stop sucking thumb." We use pictures of our goals to create vision boards that we hang in our bedrooms to remind us throughout the year of what we want to accomplish. Check out an example here: https://www.fridayfwd .com/vision-board/.

To read more inspirational stories about building your intellectual capacity, visit www.fridayfwd .com/intellectual

Scan me with your camera phone for more resources!

INTELLECTUAL

4.

Build Your Physical Capacity

"Take care of your body. It's the
only place you have to live."

—JIM ROHN

P hysical capacity is your ability to improve your
health, well-being, and physical performance.
While your brain helps drive and guide you through
life, it's your body that is asked to do most of the
heavy lifting, day in and day out.

While we understand the concept of building physical strength and endurance, we often overlook the other aspects of being healthy, particularly the connection between our brains and our bodies. Fortunately, this correlation is gaining far more awareness.

Your physical capacity acts as either an accelerant or a drag on your overall quest to build capacity. When your physical capacity is strong, you have more endurance and resilience. You rise to the occasion. You also learn and process faster (intellectual capacity) and feel better about yourself and have more to give to others (emotional capacity). When your physical capacity is not strong, doing almost anything is harder, if not impossible.

Symptoms such as fatigue and stress significantly affect your immunity and how you feel day to day. The same is true of your food choices, which serve as the fuel for both your mind and body. Often, these factors work against the other positive things you are doing to increase your physical capacity.

Your health and physical capacity are more holistic concepts than you realize.

MAINTAINING HEALTH AND WELLNESS

"The greatest gift you can give your family and the world is a healthy you."

—JOYCE MEYER

You don't see many high achievers who allow their mental or physical health to deteriorate precipitously. Sleeping, eating well, and exercise are all basic needs that should be uncompromising priorities in our lives. We know this intuitively, yet many of us ignore it or look the other way daily.

Unfortunately, your health is one of those things you don't really value until you lose it. And then one day, the phone rings. Your doctor is calling you because the tests are back and you have cancer. Or the emergency room is calling to say your partner had a heart attack. From then on, nothing is ever the same, and you wish you could turn back the clock.

I was lucky enough to get a warning shot.

In 2009, I was temporarily living with my parents while my wife and I built a new house just a few months after having our third child. We were also running two new businesses in the middle of a historical recession. Then, in the spring of 2009, my grandmother suddenly passed away.

A few weeks later, I was working from home one morning, having my second cup of coffee, when I noticed my heart was racing. A few hours later, I noticed tingling in my arm that grew increasingly pronounced. Googling my symptoms, heart attack references kept showing up, making me even more anxious.

I called my wife and told her she should come home, which was totally out of character for me. For perspective, I am the person who drives himself home from his own surgery, as another one of my core values is *self-reliance*.

My youngest son, Zach, was also home with a babysitter. Convinced I was having a heart attack, I asked her to call 911, as I was getting faint and struggling to stand. I looked into Zach's eyes from across the room, hung up the phone, and collapsed to the floor. I distinctively remember thinking, "I can't believe this is how I am going to die."

After two days of testing in the hospital, it was determined that I had suffered from a massive panic attack, triggered by stress and a magnesium deficiency that caused an increased heartbeat. Otherwise, I was totally healthy.

This experience was the wake-up call for me. Looking into my baby son's eyes and thinking he would never know his father is a memory I will never forget. I even keep the medical bracelet from my hospital stay on my desk at eye level as a reminder. Soon after, I committed to getting back into yoga and exercise and

started running for the first time in my life and paying close attention to my diet.

We've achieved a point in history where more people will die of obesity than starvation. Despite all the marvels of modern medicine, many of us are unhealthier than we've ever been. A telling statistic points to the places where the American diet of fast foods and processed foods is adopted. In these places, the big three health issues (heart disease, cancer, and diabetes) begin to appear within a decade. There is also a growing body of scientific evidence showing the connection between our guts and our brains, meaning that our food choices affect not only how we feel but also our cognitive abilities and our mental health.

Nutrition can be confusing. There are so many diets and "eating styles" now that it's hard to keep track of them, much less determine which one might work best for you. There's organic, vegan, vegetarian, keto, paleo, gluten-free, grain-free, low-carb, slow-carb, and no-carb, among others. It can be mind-bending to figure out how to eat healthy.

As a baseline, if you want to improve your eating, I suggest you follow Michael Pollan's pragmatic advice: "Don't eat anything your great-grandmother wouldn't recognize as food." If you do this for even a few weeks, I believe you will notice a profound difference in how you feel and your level of energy. In more simple terms, "real food" does not have a nutritional label.

While losing five pounds is great, I'd advocate for a lifestyle/diet that ultimately makes you feel better and have more energy. People love to assume that the way they eat is right for everyone. Some are even forceful and judgmental in the way they approach sharing that information with others. Innovations in science are now starting to disprove this one-diet-for-all theory and uncovering how personalized one's health really is. One man's medicine is another man's poison.

In terms of physical health, both strength training

and cardiovascular exercise that elevates your heart rate should be part of your ongoing routine. Many people do one or the other, but research clearly shows you need the combination of both, especially as you age and to help prevent injury.

If you have been holding on to the excuse that you are getting too old to begin running, swimming, biking, or participating in other endurance-based activities, it's time to flip that argument on its head.

The reality is that many people who were competitive athletes earlier in their lives have an uphill battle as they age due to the significant long-term wear and tear on their bodies. You may be starting from an advantage. In fact, the average triathlete is now thirty-eight years old. I ran my first Olympic triathlon at forty-one, having never run more than a mile outside of sports practice before I was thirty-five.

GETTING SLEEP AND MANAGING STRESS

*"Sleep is an investment in
the energy you need to be
effective tomorrow."*
—TOM RATH

In terms of your overall health, two of the biggest factors that will affect your capacity are sleep and stress. Recent studies from both Harvard and Washington State have shown how both stress and a lack of sleep tend to lead to poor decision-making.[5]

Most of us just aren't getting enough sleep. Moreover, we tend to cover up our sleep deficiency by using coffee and increasingly available sources of instant caffeine. While this is good for Starbucks's and food companies' bottom lines, too much of these instant uppers may lead to longer-term health issues.

In one of its annual reports, the National Sleep Foundation found that overall health was highly associated with sleep quality. Sixty-seven percent of those with less-than-good sleep quality also report poor or only fair health, with 27 percent reporting otherwise good health.[6]

Stress is also reaching epidemic levels. It's important to understand that stress is natural, but it's also an internal response to an external force. It's something your own mind and body creates; there is no universal stress trigger.

The biological purpose of stress is to address danger. In prehistoric times, stress provided a temporary boost of adrenaline and fueled short-term improvements in attention and memory to aid humans in our fight-or-flight response. The operative word is *temporary*. The problem is that today, most of us are functioning in stress mode for longer than our bodies are designed, thus generating an excess of the stress hormone cortisol. In short, chronic stress makes us sick and unhealthy.

According to Dr. Heidi Hanna, a leading expert

on stress, the biggest issue with our current stress epidemic is that most people don't fully understand what exactly is stressing them out. "In today's hyper-connected society," she wrote to me, "we have access to more stimulation and information in one day than we are wired to process in a lifetime. Because the brain is hard-wired to constantly crave more, most people struggle to disconnect and recharge even when they have time to do so."

Today, people all over the world will wake up stressed. Some will be worrying about how they'll find food or shelter for the day; others will be thinking about a big presentation they are giving for the first time. There are even those who will be legitimately stressed about coordinating the management logistics of their four multimillion-dollar homes. Regardless of the reason, they're stressed beyond a natural, healthy state.

To reduce and better manage stress, Hanna suggests building in time to regularly recharge throughout the day, whether by meditating, breathing deeply, or taking the time to reflect on things you are grateful for. Mindfulness and mediation are two popular practices with those who elevate.

One key to maintaining your health and well-being is to make sure that you are putting yourself first. When you're on a plane, just before takeoff, you'll hear, "In the case of an emergency, secure your own oxygen mask first." The airlines remind us of this on every flight, because they've learned we are more likely to focus on helping our kids first, then ourselves, which could do more harm than good in an emergency. This safety tip is really an important metaphor.

Too often, we put ourselves last and say yes to too many things and people, dividing our energy into too many disparate activities. The result is that we aren't as effective at helping others as we could be. And when time is at a premium, typically the first thing cut from the schedule is rest, relaxation, exercise, and high-quality food.

If you don't put yourself first, then everyone experiences a suboptimal version of you. Putting your physical health and well-being first isn't selfish; it's often the best thing you can do in the service of others and to ensure you will be around for them in the long term.

You only get one vehicle to take you through this life, so treat that vehicle well.

EMBRACING COMPETITION

"You are not in competition with anybody except yourself—plan to outdo your past, not other people."

—JAACHYNMA N. E. AGU

Competition is a vital part of achievement and elevating, but it's often very misunderstood and underappreciated.

We compete in most aspects of our lives on a regular basis. We compete for jobs we want, college admission spots, and for new clients and employees. The term *compete* actually comes from the Latin word *competere*, which means "strive together" and is a foundation of excellence. Individuals and teams should embrace the challenge of healthy competition and understand that it helps us each stretch our capacity, especially when we are working together as a team.

I don't know many companies that want to be the ten-thousandth-best place to work or to hire talent that no one else is interested in. In life, the reality is that you will want things that others want as well. Even the most enlightened yoga instructor competes to achieve higher certification levels and for the most prestigious teaching roles.

Competition has gotten a bad rap in the last decade as participation trophies have become ubiquitous in American culture. Today, kids participating in sports are increasingly encouraged not to keep score. The problem with the "everyone wins" mentality is that it has associated minimal effort with rewards.

Just showing up should not be met with praise and rewards. *It should be a prerequisite.*

To build both physical and intellectual capacity, we must understand the benefits that competition provides.

Competing is about elevating your own game, practicing, getting better, and giving a maximum effort. It's not about winning at all costs or wishing failure on others. In the realm of emotional capacity, you also need to learn how to both win well and lose well.

This is the true essence of competition. Great competitors make those around them better by helping to set a higher bar, regardless of whether it's in academics, music, or sports.

In basketball, Larry Bird and Magic Johnson pushed each other to be better.

Leonardo da Vinci and Michelangelo both came of age during the same era and were intense rivals.

In the 1990s, the bands Pearl Jam and Nirvana competed intensely, ultimately leading to the launch of a new era of grunge music.

We see this in business as well. Some of the most defining periods in a company or industry's journey is when competition is most acute. Bill Gates and Steve Jobs always had to compete head-to-head as they knew their industry made it impossible to rest on success for very long. This competition added value to users in the PC revolution.

Industries without competition become monopolies. Monopolies don't innovate; they become complacent and only do the minimum they need to get by. It's only when new competitors come in that the incumbent players wake up and start focusing on driving change.

One founder and CEO, Josh Linkner, actually invented a fake competitor for his company HelloWorld

called Slither and even sent out a fake press release about Slither's success to his team. He credited this competitor with helping his team to avoid complacency and maintain urgency.[7]

Elevating competition is also not just about having external rivals. It also occurs at a healthy level within the best teams.

BUILDING RESILIENCY

"The greatest glory in living
lies not in never falling but in
rising every time we fall."

—OLIVER GOLDSMITH

Resilience is a critical ingredient in capacity building. Rarely is your path to high achievement clear or straight, nor does it unfold seamlessly without setbacks along the way. In fact, how you achieve new heights is often directly correlated with both the mental and physical obstacles you overcome in the process.

There is a very compelling chicken and egg debate about resiliency and whether it is physical or emotional in origin and nature. It is partly both, for sure, but I believe that first overcoming *physical* obstacles and growing physical capacity is the catalyst for increased emotional capacity, which then becomes a virtuous circle.

Alex Hutchinson, who has studied the science of endurance for many years, says, "What a lot of endurance activities have in common is that you have to hold your finger in the flame. You have to resist your impulse to pull it away, whatever your first impulse is. That's a unifying theme that brings together great athletes and great performers in business and other contexts."

A few years back, my middle son panicked in the middle of a ropes course obstacle. He was scared and wanted me to come get him down, as did many of the parents who were watching. Rather than rescue him, I thought it was important that he make it through on his own, so I calmly talked him through how to complete the obstacle, which he did.

Was he happy with me at the time? Of course not. But the next time we went to that same ropes course, he flew through that same challenge without hesitation and led his friends through it as well. That sense of physical achievement translated into confidence in other areas of his life.

Behind each story of achievement, you will find many untold stories of failure and adversity that needed to be overcome. In this life, you will face unexpected setbacks; it's just a matter of how you respond and if you keep going.

One of the interesting aspects of resilience is the timeline.

Some situations will call for you to be resilient over a day or a week, while other circumstances require you to maintain that resilience for an entire period of your life in order to make it through to the other side.

For most of us, it is actually the lowest points that define our character and resolve and help us clarify what we want most in life. Failure and struggle are the path to success, not an obstacle.

This leads to the question: When are you most resilient?

You are most resilient when you have developed your spiritual capacity so that you are clear about

your core values and purpose and feel you are doing something that must be done.

Think about all the famous figures in history who were willing to die for the cause(s) they believed in most.

If you don't really want to fight for it, you need to be willing to give up and move on without guilt to apply that energy elsewhere.

Elizabeth Edwards summed this up best in her memoir, *Saving Graces: Finding Solace and Strength from Friends and Strangers*. As she bravely fought brain cancer and faced an embarrassing affair by her husband, a prominent U.S. senator, she wrote, "Part of resilience is deciding to make yourself miserable over something that matters or deciding to make yourself miserable over something that doesn't matter."

ACTION STEPS

Getting Started

▶ Take two fifteen-minute breaks during the day, preferably outdoors and without any technology.

▶ Get eight hours of sleep—tonight!

▶ Download a meditation app (e.g., Headspace or Calm), and try a free, guided meditation for five to ten minutes. See the QR code below for more options.

▶ If you have never run before, download the Couch to 5K app (https://www.active.com/mobile/couch-to-5k-app).

Advanced

▶ Sign up for an event that you haven't done before (i.e., 5K, bike ride, Tough Mudder, Spartan Race, triathlon) that will take at least two to three months of training.

▶ Commit to not using technology for the first hour after you wake up and the last hour before you go to sleep. Use the built-in functions on your Android or iPhone to restrict your phone overnight automatically.

▶ Sign up for an intramural team sport, which provides physical exercise, competition, and connection.

▶ If you really want to push your limits, check out the online and in-person programs from the High Performance Institute (https://www.jjhpi.com/).

To read more inspirational stories about building your physical capacity, visit www.fridayfwd.com/physical

Scan me with your camera phone for more resources!

PHYSICAL

5.

Build Your Emotional Capacity

"No one succeeds alone, gains freedom alone, or finds joy alone."

—ADAM GRANT

Your level of emotional capacity is deeply connected with how you manage the little voice in your head, interact with others, and the quality of your relationships.

When you see two people of seemingly equal intellectual and physical capacity achieving very different outcomes, it is quite likely due to an imbalance in emotional capacity.

None of us exist in a vacuum. We live in a world in which our actions, interactions, and experiences are interwoven into the lives and actions of others. The quality of our relationships and the energy gained or consumed by these relationships is extremely powerful.

Think about a race car. If your spiritual, physical, and intellectual capacities are the tools to design, build, and improve the car, your emotional capacity is your ability to actually drive it in the presence of other drivers and unintended obstacles.

How you react and relate to the other cars will ultimately determine if your car performs above or below its factory specifications.

For most of us, it is the missing piece in our quest to build capacity and is often the most difficult, because it extends beyond the control of our own four walls.

OVERCOMING SELF-LIMITING BELIEFS

"Our deepest fear is not that we are inadequate. Our deepest fear is that we are powerful beyond measure. It is our light, not our darkness that most frightens us."

—MARIANNE WILLIAMSON

The first step in building your emotional capacity begins when you learn to stop doubting yourself and you realize that many of your limits are self-imposed. If you are clear about your purpose and values, you would think it would be easy to live by them. But it's not, is it?

Too often, we are held back by our own self-limiting beliefs, as well as the expectations created for us by others. This cycle goes on within us each day, often without us even realizing it.

Instead of acknowledging and pursuing our true potential, it's far more convenient (and less frightening) to manufacture reasons we can't do something. What we really fear is doing the work that is necessary. For years, I knew I wanted to write a book. In 2016, I was sitting in class as part of a three-year entrepreneurial leadership program and had finally made the decision that I was going to write a book before we met the next year. That small change in my language and thinking from "I *want* to write a book" to "I *am going* to write a book" changed everything. From that point on, my energy went into the how. Twelve months later, I published my first book, *Performance Partnerships*.

I now take the same approach with each of my kids, explaining that they can achieve anything they desire (spiritual capacity) if they are willing to do what's required (intellectual, physical, and emotional capacity) and make the decision to commit.

Your limiting beliefs can come from within, but often they originate from a variety of institutions and people around you—even those closest to you. This often manifests in the form of a powerful force called cognitive dissonance, the internal conflict that results from holding incongruous beliefs and attitudes at the same time. Once you understand it, you will see it everywhere.

For example, if a friend tells me I shouldn't attempt to write a book because it's too hard, it's likely that his opinion has nothing to do with me or my ability. Instead, he is very likely trying to feel better about not writing a book himself, either because he questions his own ability, or he believes that he would be more qualified than me to do it but is actually afraid to try.

When someone tries to bring you down or discourage you, it may not be malicious. That person needs to feel better about herself and the decisions she has made or avoided. She is trying to bring you to her level of capacity, due to her cognitive dissonance. Cognitive dissonance causes us to try and rationalize two contradictory or inconsistent beliefs in our heads at the same

time (i.e., I am smarter than him, therefore he can't write a book if I can't.).

The key is to remember that deep down, you know what you want, and then put your energy into getting there.

It's easier and more convenient to make excuses. It's more difficult—and far more rewarding—to believe you are fully in control of your own destiny.

You only get one shot at life. Shouldn't you give it your best, have no regrets, and leave nothing in reserve when you cross the finish line?

DISCOMFORT AND CHALLENGE

"He or she who is willing to be the most uncomfortable is not only the bravest but rises the fastest."

—BRENÉ BROWN

There is no better or faster way to overcome self-limiting believes than to constantly force yourself outside of your comfort zone or to be pushed there by others. In fact, your comfort zone is by definition the glass ceiling of your limiting believes.

None of us grows unless we're pushed a little. Think about someone in your life who has helped you grow. It may have been a parent, teacher, boss, colleague, friend, personal trainer, or a sports or business coach. Chances are that person told you what you needed

to hear, not necessarily what you wanted to hear, even when the advice frustrated you or made you angry and resentful, and that made all the difference in the world.

In living my core purpose authentically, I have grown comfortable with taking personal risks to make those I care about a little bit uncomfortable in the service of building capacity. I am definitely not the leader, coach, friend, child, spouse, or parent who is going to tell you what you want to hear just because it's easier or helps you justify your existing position. It's not who I am.

If you want that type of advice, you know the people in your own life to go to, but they won't help you grow. My friend Dr. Abdul-Malik Muhammad, who has worked for decades with at-risk youth, has identified what he believes is the formula for sparking change in others, and it represents several principles of emotional capacity.

Connection + Challenge = CHANGE

The implication of this formula is that real change only happens when you are challenged. In some cases, the challenge is what builds the connection or respect. In others, the connection is required first to earn the right to challenge, but it is the combination that ultimately drives change. When I first saw this formula, I realized it was the reason for the success of Friday Forward.

Getting out of both your mental and physical comfort zones is absolutely critical to growth. As your activities, geography, and conversations change, so do your expectations and your relationships You start to meet new people and think and act in new and different ways. As the saying goes, "If you always do what you've always done, you always get what you've always gotten."

The process of getting out of your comfort zone almost always begins with learning to be more vulnerable. You have to open up a little and let people see your weak spots. We all have them, and acknowledging you're not perfect is a necessary first step to becoming self-aware, learning, and growing.

When you artificially suppress discomfort and vulnerability, you end up creating a false sense of reality for yourself and others. You also tend to give in to many of the self-limiting beliefs that hold you back. In contrast, displaying and sharing your own vulnerabilities opens the doors for those around you to explore theirs, enabling everyone to grow together.

For our annual company retreat this past year, I invited author JT McCormick to speak to our team. JT was born the mixed-race son of a drug-dealing pimp father and an orphaned, single mother on welfare. He was raised in poverty, suffered incredible abuse (sexual and physical) and racism, and had multiple stints in the juvenile justice system. He speaks honestly and openly about his story and struggles on the path to becoming the incredible father, man, and CEO he is today. The vulnerable and authentic sharing that happened between our team members at the retreat following his speech was like nothing I had ever seen before.

One of the reasons vulnerability is harder to express these days is that we are all inundated with carefully curated social media posts that spotlight the top five percent of people's lives. This lens tends to omit the struggles, frustrations, and realities of life, which causes us—and arguably a whole generation—to compare our actual lives to a storybook version of others' lives.

For young people, another major barrier to vulnerability has been the rise of helicopter parenting, an unhealthy habit of parents who can't handle unhappy kids or accept the necessary struggle that comes with growth. These parents have taken the concept of wanting better for their children's lives far past the point of diminishing return. As such, they constantly interfere and save their kids from the pain of failure or struggle.

This behavior presents a serious and growing

threat to an entire generation of kids. As they grow up, they are unprepared for the real adversities they will face as adults. It is a problem that is now expanding generationally into a new phenomenon: helicopter *grandparenting*.

To find their own way, children must be empowered to understand their strengths and weaknesses and to learn from failure. Developing resilience is an essential element of emotional capacity and can only come from being pushed outside of one's limits and comfort zone.

Your quest to elevate requires sharing your insecurities and figuring things out for yourself. It's a trial and error process, and it can be painful. But studies show that the hint of anxiety that comes with trying something new can actually enhance performance.[8]

Maybe that's why Tony Robbins takes an ice-cold bath every morning, giving a shock to his system. He says he does it to be mentally and physically prepared to handle anything that comes at him that day.

While you might not want to jump into an ice bath, there are small yet powerful ways you can begin getting out of your comfort zone. For example, try adventurous new dishes, or attend a social event where you don't know anyone. Then begin to take on bigger challenges, both physical and mental. Do things that scare you a little. This could be making a cold call, being honest with a coworker about her poor presentation, or even asking someone out on a date who you think is a long shot.

Traveling, adapting to a new physical environment and culture, getting a little bit lost, trying to learn another language, or simply walking on a different side of the street can all shake things up and start to make you more comfortable and confident under new or unpredictable circumstances by disengaging autopilot.

A mastermind group is also a great way to build your emotional capacity in addition to your intellectual capacity. I am in a business mastermind group with very driven, goal-oriented members who are

all voracious capacity builders. Someone is always setting a new business or fitness goal for themselves, whether it's for a race, a triathlon, etc. Just being part of this group encourages me to want to keep up and to push the edges of my own comfort zone, both mentally and physically.

Real freedom comes from not bottling up your fears and insecurities. Deep down, most of us do want and need to be uncomfortable, and we all want to grow.

But you don't get one without the other.

ATTITUDE AND GRATITUDE

"Nothing can stop the man with the right mental attitude from achieving his goal; nothing on earth can help the man with the wrong mental attitude."

—ANONYMOUS

One of my mentors, Warren Rustand, loves to share a story of two people. The first person throws back the covers, jumps out of bed, and says, "Good morning, Lord." The other person peeks out from under the covers and says, "Good Lord, it's morning."

I have yet to meet a high achiever or a world-class performer who has a negative attitude or believes the worst is going to happen. Having a positive attitude doesn't mean everything will work out how you want it to, but it enables you to have the mindset required for success and to get through the inevitable mental and physical adversities that will arise along the way.

In trying to understand who would drop out of West Point in her research for her book *Grit: The Power of Passion and Perseverance*, Angela Duckworth learned from a military psychologist and West Point faculty member that the aptitude tests used for admission had little correlation to who would quit. Those who made it through had vowed not to give up, they knew what they wanted most (spiritual capacity). Similar conclusions have been drawn from research into other elite military training programs such as the Navy SEALS BUD/S training, where only 25 percent of SEAL candidates make it through Hell Week. It's not the strongest or smartest who survive. It's those who refuse to quit, and they don't quit because they are clear about what's most important to them.

It's important to acknowledge that being positive is not about unicorns and rainbows or approaching every situation with rose-colored glasses. It's more about approaching an opportunity pragmatically and seeing challenges as opportunities.

Most great businesses were born out of a frustration that the entrepreneur wanted to overcome. Rather than spending their lives complaining about the situation like everyone else and draining emotional capacity, they chose to put their energy into solving the problem.

Think about all the people in your life who assume the worst in everything and everyone. Are they high achievers? Are they happy? Do they positively impact others? Or do they love playing the role of the victim and strive to bring those around them down to their level of capacity?

Your attitude in life is also strongly correlated with how much you focus on yourself relative to other people. For instance, it is difficult to be angry or fearful while you are grateful. This is because anger and fear are self-focused, whereas gratitude is about focusing beyond yourself.

A big part of having a positive attitude revolves around living in the present, something most people find increasingly difficult to do. Rather, they often find themselves reflecting on what might have been or having anxiety about what will come next. As one popular saying goes, "If you are depressed, you are living in the past. If you are anxious, you are living in the future. If you are at peace, you are living in the present."

People who live in the present are fundamentally grateful for what they have in that movement. People who are grateful also don't feel that the world owes them anything. They believe it's their responsibility to go out and get it.

Kids who grow up entitled and ungrateful feel that things should come to them easily. They tend to worry more about what they don't have and that others do. They also often struggle and become easily depressed when things don't go their way.

There is a philosophical view that suffering is a result of an intense focus on one's self. Gratitude moves you away from this suffering and toward appreciation for what you have. It shifts you into a state of presence, which is your healthiest state.

True gratefulness also creates a deeper connection to others, and it is those relationships that will play such critical roles in your ultimate success and happiness.

MEANINGFUL RELATIONSHIPS

"The quality of your life is determined by the quality of your relationships."

—TONY ROBBINS

Study after study has shown that money doesn't make you happier, nor does it make you live longer. The one thing that has proven to accomplish both is having quality relationships in your life. Experiencing positive, fulfilling relationships and being surrounded by others who bring out the best in you are cornerstones of building capacity and happiness. Great relationships encourage you to be better and give you energy. They also provide a support structure and make you healthier, touching every element of capacity building. Conversely, poor relationships have the inverse effect.

In the early days of building Acceleration Partners, I realized that quality relationships would be a foundation of our success, so we decided to make *embracing relationships* one of our core values. Here is how we defined it:

Relationships advance our personal and professional lives, contributing greatly to our successes. We focus on long-term outcomes, meaningful relationships, and genuine connections with our clients, teammates, and partners. We believe that competence and character are fundamental to relationships built on trust and that quality relationships allow us to achieve more.

A good friend once told me that a formula for success in life is *what* you know raised to the power of *who* you know (What^{Who}). I wholeheartedly agree with this. Personal knowledge is far less valuable if you don't have a way to connect with others to apply it. What's interesting is that in this equation, the who actually has the logarithmic or multiplicative effect, meaning that your relationships might matter more than what you know.

Most of what I have accomplished in life and in business has been because of the assistance and support of others. I credit Keith Ferrazzi and the principles he espoused in his bestselling book *Never Eat Alone*, as well as Dale Carnegie's timeless classic *How to Win Friends and Influence People*, for how I have approached networking and relationship building. Both taught me to focus on the needs of others and the creation of values for others.

If you ever find yourself considering joining a business or starting a new venture with a partner, I would encourage you to think far more about who you are going to be working with than what the company does. The product or idea won't matter if you wake up every day and have to spend time with people you don't enjoy or respect. Every time someone asks me for advice on choosing one opportunity over another, I immediately focus on the people and the relationships.

In terms of your personal relationships, as you grow your capacity, it'll become even more important for you to be discerning about who you spend your time with and the effort you want to put into continuing or exiting certain relationships.

Once you've discovered your core purpose and implemented your core values in your daily life, you can more easily identify the people who share your values and those who don't. It is vital to be intentional about surrounding yourself with like-minded people who can help you grow and fulfill your potential.

As Jim Rohn once said, "You are the average of the five people you spend the most time with." I can't think of a more powerful statement. You should want to surround yourself with people who energize you and help you to be your best self, so that you are being pulled forward and not held back.

If you aren't yet convinced that capacity building is the path to achievement, think about someone who does exactly the opposite; let's call him Steve.

Steve doesn't have a clear sense of who he is or what he wants. He also doesn't believe he can improve. He is overweight, easts poorly, doesn't exercise, and drinks too much. He doesn't compete, because he's afraid to lose, and never tries anything new. Steve alienates many friends and family and hangs around with people who bring him down and reinforce his existing beliefs.

Do you know *anyone* like Steve in your life who is a high achiever or who is focused on elevating themselves?

The answer is no. And you probably don't want to hang around a lot of Steves either.

Think about the five people who you associate with the most today. Do they help you build your capacity? Or do they pull you down to their level of mediocrity? If you want to elevate, but you realize you are the smartest person in the room, it may be time to switch rooms.

It's always good to engage with people who have different viewpoints where you can respectfully disagree on subjects and gain perspective. However, when you really start to build your spiritual and intellectual capacity and identify what you want from life, you will face some hard choices. Your standards will rise, and this will impact existing friendships and social circles. You will find it much harder to be with or give valuable energy to people who aren't aligned to your values or goals. For example, I have a really hard time being around people whose demonstrated values clash with or are the antithesis of my own. If I meet someone who has no interest in becoming better (a core value of mine)—someone who tells me they could never change, always blames external factors, and constantly positions themselves as a victim—I really can't be around them for long. It feels like kryptonite.

You will need to make the difficult decision to walk away from relationships that are not helping you get to where you want to be and rid your life of "energy vampires."

This might include some longtime friends or relationships that never had much depth and have run their course, and it gets incredibly difficult if you realize that family members are some of the people you need to stop from draining your energy. Family is very important, but I don't believe it should be an absolute.

When dealing with a family member who is always bringing you down, don't assume they will change. They will only change if *they* want to change. Your remaining choices are to change your reaction to their behavior or walk away.

This transition may require some of the toughest

choices you've ever had to make. But it doesn't mean burning bridges or starting fights—actions that are counterproductive to building emotional capacity. Simply deemphasize some of these relationships. Simply stop engaging, making plans, or giving that relationship much of your precious time and energy.

At this point in my life, I have become much more focused on relationships of significance. One meaningful, fulfilling relationship in my life is worth ten or twenty casual ones.

The process of evaluating and changing your relationships may take years of intentional thought, very difficult decisions, and life changes. However, cultivating the right relationships in your life, as well as pruning the ones have been holding you back, is one of the most important things you can do in your life to build your capacity and elevate.

ACTION STEPS

Getting Started

▶ Do something small that changes your daily routine.
  Some options:

- Eat lunch at a different place.

- Walk home or to work a different way.

- Change your start or end time by a few hours.

▶ Share something on social media that demonstrates
  vulnerability. It could be a struggle, a fear, or a
  frustration.

▶ Make a list of the five most important personal and
  professional relationships in your life and put it on your
  desk.

Advanced

▶ Sign up for an activity you have never done before that
  has an entry fee and a due date. This will also advance
  several other areas of capacity building.

- Pick something you have previously thought that you could not do, ask yourself why, and then keep asking why each time you answer (up to five times). Then propose a solution to each answer.

- Create a "relationships dashboard" of the thirty most important people in your life and pick one name each day to reach out to. It could be a call, email, or even a handwritten note.

- If you want to learn more about the power of cognitive dissonance, I strongly suggest reading *Mistakes Were Made (But Not by Me): Why We Justify Foolish Beliefs, Bad Decisions, and Hurtful Acts* by Carol Tavris and Elliot Aronson. It is one of the most important books on relationships and mindset I have read.

To read more inspirational stories about building your emotional capacity, visit www.fridayfwd .com/emotional.

Scan me with your camera phone for more resources!

EMOTIONAL

6.

Build a Better Path

"Be the person you needed when you were younger."

—AYESHA SIDDIQI

This is a quote that resonates with me deeply. When you are struggling to discover your core purpose, I would suggest you explore and reflect on your past, as it is often where the answers lie.

I have very few regrets in life, but my biggest is

knowing that I spent a large portion of my time on this earth being an underachiever rather than an outperformer. Deep down, I always knew I could elevate myself, that I could do better. I just didn't know how or why.

I am definitely not an overnight success (and by my own standards, I'm not even prepared to say I am a success). However, it's important to share that the path to greater achievement has been bumpy. It has taken many years to clarify and align to my core values. I still make plenty of mistakes, and some of my decisions have led to big misses. I am far from where I want to be, but I am committed to get there through the process of capacity building and leading others to do the same.

Here's a snapshot of me at age five, recounted by my preschool teacher:

Although he is a keen observer of detail and has proven he is most capable in many areas, he also makes it quite clear that he would rather be doing something else. He seems much more interested in exploring the cause and effect of things. It is our hope that he will continue to be provided with the material and opportunities to stimulate the challenge of his creative mind to his potential.

Even though I went to good schools, this "stimulation" didn't pan out until much later in my life. I was often bored in class. My teachers frequently commented that I wasn't living up to my ability; it was a recurring theme. The problem was no one provided the inspiration or the how. They focused on what I did not do well, such as focus, instead of what I was good at—creativity and leadership.

I think it's common for people like me to feel confused, frustrated, misunderstood, and alone as a kid, because cultural norms encourage us to conform and keep up with the Joneses. Like many other curious

and entrepreneurial kids, I found the conventional path unappealing.

Entrepreneurial and business success stories are often told through rose-colored glasses. Entrepreneurship, in particular, seems much simpler and more exciting when looked at in the rearview mirror. Rarely, however, is that view a true representation of the years of struggle, sacrifice, and failure that typically precede achievements.

There are few, if any, institutions in our society that provide students with access to mentors and inspiration that both recognizes and prepares kids for leadership and entrepreneurship. Most education systems reward conformity when they would do better to take inventory of young people's strengths and weaknesses, help them discover their purpose(s), inspire them, and push them to grow their capacity in a way that makes sense for them.

Instead, many kids encounter teachers who paint innate strengths as weaknesses. These might be strengths like independent-mindedness or nonconformity. Bestselling author Seth Godin calls this the "curse of the cog." He goes on to say that, "Since you were five, schools and society have been teaching you to be a cog in the machine of our economy. To do what you're told, to sit in straight lines, and to get the work done."[9]

The school valedictorian and the prom queen/king are, in many ways, the ultimate conformists. It's why they win the first leg of the race but often underachieve in the long run. The reason is that a very specific set of conforming behaviors were rewarded. Many leaders and entrepreneurs are just not comfortable conforming, even as children. Conforming does not serve them, and it prevents society from benefitting from the different perspective needed to make big changes.

There simply aren't enough people or organizations who would take a child and say, "Look, you're different. We can see the potential you have. Let us teach you how to be a leader. Let us teach you how to push the envelope and break the rules that limit your potential. Let us teach you how to use your talents to be the exception."

That's why the mission of the nonprofit organization BUILD resonates so deeply with me and why I am donating a percentage of the profits of this book to the organization.

BUILD identifies self-driven and underserved high school students; provides them with the inspiration, skills, actual experience, and mentorship necessary for success; and connects them with business leaders. As its name signifies, it's an organization focused on building kids up and increasing their capacity across each of the four elements of capacity building.

For students in the BUILD program who stay with it for all four years of high school, the graduation rate is close to *95 percent*. Compare that to approximately sixty percent for non-BUILD students at the same schools. It's a controlled study on the power of capacity building.

Thinking back to my days as an underperforming and unengaged high school student, I would have loved a program like BUILD. With this book—and the organization it supports—my goal is to carve out an inspiring, resource-rich path for future leaders and entrepreneurs.

What I've eventually realized is that I am trying to be the person I needed when I was younger, and this has become the driving force behind the way I live my life, lead, and develop the next generation of leaders in my business. I am all in on capacity building.

We all have infinitely more capacity than we believe. We also need to be champions of building capacity in others, including our children, friends, family, coworkers, and employees. No one should be living up to less than their full potential.

And it starts with you.

Start by having high expectations for yourself. As you build your capacity, you will naturally inspire the same behavior in others, multiplying your impact.

Remember, great leaders don't create followers. They create more leaders.[10]

Stop underachieving. Hold yourself and others accountable, and commit to living life to your full potential.

It's time to elevate!

Notes

1   Stephanie Rosenbloom, "The World According to Tim Ferriss," *New York Times*, March 25, 2011, https://www.nytimes.com/2011/03/27/fashion/27Ferris.html?src=twrhp.

2   Jeffrey Pfeffer, "What You Can Learn from Tim Ferriss about Power," *Harvard Business Review*, March 29, 2011, https://hbr.org/2011/03/power-comes-to-those-willing-t.

3   Kim Scott, *Radical Candor: Be a Kick-Ass Boss Without Losing Your Humanity* (New York: St. Martin's Press, 2017), 21.

4   Charles Duhigg coined the term keystone habit in his book *The Power of Habit: Why We Do What We Do in Life and Business* (New York: Random House, 2012).

5   Will Ferguson, "Research Shows Sleep Loss Impedes Decision Making in Crisis," *WSU Insider*, May 7, 2015, https://news .wsu.edu/2015/05/07/research-shows-sleep-loss-impedes -decision-making-in-crisis/; Ron Carucci, "Stress Leads to Bad Decisions. Here's How to Avoid Them," *Harvard Business Review*, August 29, 2017, https://hbr.org/2017/08/stress-leads-to-bad -decisions-heres-how-to-avoid-them.

6   "Lack of Sleep Is Affecting Americans, Finds the National Sleep Foundation," National Sleep Foundation, December 2014, https://www.sleepfoundation.org/press-release/lack-sleep -affecting-americans-finds-national-sleep-foundation.

7   Leigh Buchanan, "How I Did It: Josh Linkner, CEO, ePrize," Inc.com, September 1, 2006, https://www.inc.com/magazine /20060901/hidi-linkner.html.

8   Melinda Beck, "Anxiety Can Bring Out the Best," *Wall Street Journal*, June 18, 2012, https://www.wsj.com/articles/SB1000 142405270230383640457747 44451463041994.

9   Seth Godin, "The Ever-Worsening Curse of the Cog," Seth's Blog, March 2, 2005, https://seths.blog/2005/03/the _everworseni/.

10   Tom Peters, "Rule #3: Leadership Is Confusing as Hell," *Fast Company*, February 28, 2001, https://www.fastcompany .com/42575/rule-3-leadership-confusing-hell.

Acknowledgments

I have many people to thank who were part of my journey to writing this book. I apologize in advance to anyone left out inadvertently.

First to my parents, who gave me the independence I needed from a very early age to forge my own path in life and learn from my mistakes.

To all those who have provided mentoring and guidance and pushed me to be better, including John Gifford, Tom Warren, Arun Gupta, Sarah DiTroia, Tim Rowe, Natan Parsons, Cam Herold, Steve Tritman, and my Acceleration Partners board.

To the amazing leaders and peers I have met though Entrepreneurs' Organization (EO), an organization that has changed the trajectory of my life. This includes my forum, my Leadership Academy Class of 2013, and my EMP Class of 2018. To Fletch and Carlo and the Leadership Academy Class of 2015 for inspiring me to make the next step with Friday Forward.

To Warren Rustand, who, more than anyone I have ever met, has helped me and countless others discover our purpose, increase our expectations for ourselves, and live to our fullest potential.

To Lenox Powell, my sounding board for writing and diligent Friday Forward editor. Each week, she helps turn my run-on sentences and typos into a clear and polished end product that makes a real impact.

To my personal board of editors including Alex Yastrebenetsky, Brad Pedersen, Rob Dube, Chris Hutchinson, and Jeff Haden, for giving me your time and your honest feedback.

To Brad, Ellie, JT, Tucker, and the Scribe Media

team for all their support and hard work in bringing the book to life.

To my agent, Rick Pascocello, who pushed me to create a story from what was originally an idea for a compilation. Thanks for taking a chance on me and for believing in the impact of my writing. I am forever grateful.

To my editor, Meg Gibbons, who has always enthusiastically been in my corner. And to the entire Sourcebooks team for their support and excitement through the process, from start to finish.

And last but never least, to my wife, Rachel. In 1999, when I was only twenty-three years old, she gave me a copy of Patrick Lencioni's *Five Temptations of a CEO* after hearing him speak at a conference. This was the first book that inspired me to want more and think about my own capacity to lead. As part of writing this book, I recently decided to revisit the *Five Temptations of a CEO*, which has rested quietly upon my bookshelf for the past eighteen years since I first read it. When I reopened the book, I was touched to rediscover a note Rachel had written to me inside the front cover. The note ended with:

"I truly believe that you have the qualities that it takes to be a great CEO, and I do not doubt for one minute that you will achieve that goal."

We all need someone to believe in us, and as it turns out, she may have been the source of my inspiration all along.

About the Author

ROBERT GLAZER is the founder and CEO of global performance marketing agency Acceleration Partners. A serial entrepreneur, Bob has a passion for helping individuals and organizations build their capacity to elevate.

Under his leadership, Acceleration Partners has received numerous industry and company culture awards, including Glassdoor's Employees' Choice Awards (two years in a row), *Ad Age*'s Best Place to

Work, *Entrepreneur*'s Top Company Culture (two years in a row), Great Place to Work and *Fortune*'s Best Small and Medium Workplaces (three years in a row), and *Boston Globe*'s Top Workplaces (two years in a row). Bob was also named to Glassdoor's list of Top CEO of Small and Medium Companies in the U.S., ranking number two.

A regular columnist for *Forbes* and *Entrepreneur*, Bob's writing reaches over five million people around the globe each year who resonate with his topics, which range from performance marketing and entrepreneurship to company culture, capacity building, hiring, and leadership. Worldwide, he is also a sought-after speaker by companies and organizations on subjects related to business growth, culture, building capacity, and performance.

Bob shares his ideas and insights via Friday Forward, a popular weekly inspirational newsletter that reaches over one hundred thousand individuals and business leaders across over fifty countries. He is also the author of the international bestselling book *Performance Partnerships*.

Outside of work, Bob can likely be found skiing, cycling, reading, traveling, spending quality time with his family, or overseeing some sort of home renovation project.

Learn more about Bob at robertglazer.com.

ABOUT BUILD

My goal in writing this book was to help people improve their lives and the lives of those around them. In purchasing this book, you've already contributed to both of those goals.

First, you've set the wheels in motion to improve your own life.

Second, you've helped improve the lives of underserved high school students via an organization named BUILD. A percent of all proceeds from this book will directly benefit the life-changing work of this program, which works to get students into college by giving them the resources necessary for achievement in entrepreneurship, college, careers, and life, through the same concept of capacity building.

BUILD participants' lives are transformed from the impact of mentors who invest time in them, believe in them, and encourage them to increase their capacity. BUILD changes the lives of these students and, in turn, changes the trajectory of future generations.

If you'd like to become further involved with BUILD's unique entrepreneurship program, you can visit their national website at Build.org to see the many ways to contribute to their nationwide mission or find a local chapter near you. You can be a donor, mentor, business coach, tutor, or more.

I am always interested in new ideas, partnerships, and feedback and would love to hear from you. Feel free to drop a line at elevate@robertglazer.com. I work to read every e-mail and respond to most.

Additional Resources:

For additional resources, links, and more detail on how to grow your goals, please visit www.fridayfwd.com/action.

The official *Elevate* book site:

robertglazer.com/elevate

More about me:

robertglazer.com

About my company:

http://www.accelerationpartners.com

NEW! Only from Simple Truths®

IGNITE READS
spark impact in just one hour

IGNITE READS IS A NEW SERIES OF 1-HOUR READS WRITTEN BY WORLD-RENOWNED EXPERTS!

These captivating books will help you become the best version of yourself, allowing for new opportunities in your personal and professional life. Accelerate your career and expand your knowledge with these powerful books written on today's hottest ideas.

TRENDING BUSINESS AND PERSONAL GROWTH TOPICS

 Read in an hour or less

 Leading experts and authors

 Bold design and captivating content